WILL CARLING'S
ENGLAND DREAM TEAM

WILL CARLING'S
ENGLAND DREAM TEAM

WILL CARLING

with additional text by
NIGEL BLUNDELL

SUNBURST BOOKS

Acknowledgements
Picture Credits: Action Images Sports Picture Agnecy:
Pages 3, 4, 5, 16, 17, 24, 30, 31, 40, 41, 43, 44, 46, 49, 50, 52, 53,
54, 55, 57, 58, 60, 61, 63, 64, 68, 69, 70, 75, 76, 77

Richard Sharp:
Pages 34, 35.

Clive Woodward:
Page 70.

This edition first published in 1996 by
Sunburst Books,
Deacon House,
65 Old Church Street,
London SW3 5BS

© Revelation Publishing Ltd 1996

Edited by
Eric Tompson
Designed by
Clearest Communications Ltd

Every effort has been made to trace the ownership of all copyrighted material
and to secure permission from copyright holders. In the event of any question
arising as to the use of any material we will be pleased to make the necessary
corrections in future printings.

ISBN 1 85778 246 1

Printed and bound in the United Kingdom

CONTENTS

PREFACE

It was a daunting challenge for England Rugby captain Will Carling – to pick an English Dream Team from all the game's greats of today and yesteryear.

In Will's own words, the task was as impossible as stopping Jonah Lomu in his tracks!

And Will knew that whatever team he picked, it would be a controversial choice.

For instance, is Rob Andrew the greatest fly half England have ever seen? Is Brian Moore the best hooker, or Rory Underwood the greatest winger?

All are great England players of today, winning Five Nation Championships and leading assaults on the Rugby World Cup. But are they good enough to grace the Dream Team? Are they the greatest players England has ever produced? Have there been stronger or faster players who would have stopped the dreaded Lomu and brought home the World Cup in 1995?

Only one man is in a position to know. If he could have changed time, who would he have taken with him on his crucial international challenges? More to the point, who would he pick tomorrow to face the might of the world's best? Over the following pages you will discover the answer ... as the most successful England rugby captain of all time picks his country's fantasy squad.

So who, after all the agonies of deliberation, did our England hero choose? Will, it's over to you to tell us how you tackled the toughest tactical challenge of your career...

At some time or other YOU must have chosen your own England 'Dream Team'. Well now it's my turn! In this book you are about to encounter – and see in action – some of the finest rugby players ever to don an England International shirt.

I have known ever since I sat down with my selector's pencil and my list of the all-time greats that, whatever team I chose, it would be a controversial selection. My choice will be long debated, down to each of the 15 positions.

I'm sure you will disagree with me – perhaps violently – over some (or all!) of my famous Fifteen. And there are, of course, omissions. They may perhaps shock you. But remember, I am dealing with a unique band of all-time golden greats knitted together in a team that may be pure fiction ... but must also be pure magic.

To help me make my selection, I went to rugby union's spiritual home, Twickenham. I wandered across rugby's most hallowed turf, soaking in the magical atmosphere — and the 'ghosts' of the champions who have trodden it.

'Twickers' has been the home of English rugby since 1910. The supreme exponents of the game have left their mark there. That fact alone made me realise that the task of choosing my final Fifteen would be almost as impossible as stopping Jonah Lomu in his tracks! My first instinct was to draw all my closest friends. But that wouldn't have solved anything. So I had to sit down and think to myself: what style of rugby would I really like to play? Then I made my judgment about the team.

Here, then, is the final line-up — a selection I have agonised over but am finally confident with. Study them, please. Then I'll try to answer the sort of questions all lovers of the game will want to ask me about my very personal Dream Team.

THE TEAM

Full Back	15	Mike Catt
Right Wing	14	David Duckham
Centre	13	Jeremy Guscott
Centre	12	Clive Woodward
Left Wing	11	Rory Underwood
Fly Half	10	Richard Sharp
Scrum Half	9	Nigel Melville
Number Eight	8	Dean Richards
Open-Side Flanker	7	Peter Winterbottom
Blind-Side Flanker	6	Jon Hall
Lock	5	Paul Ackford
Lock	4	Martin Johnson
Prop	3	Jason Leonard
Hooker	2	Peter Wheeler
Prop	1	Fran Cotton

Will Carling

THE BIG QUESTION

So why did I pick them? There must be names on that list of the Will Carling Dream Team that make you ask me that question. And there are some names I have left out that probably make you feel I have flipped.

Let me explain…

There was, as I'm sure you'll agree, a vast fund of talent to choose from – so many players who are just so incredibly good. So I had to sit down and think to myself: what style of rugby would I like to play?

I wanted to go for a dynamic running side, but one that would still win first-phase possession. I wanted an exciting, running backline. That's why I went for the half-backs I have picked. It was the same with the forwards. I chose good, solid ball-winning capabilities. I think you have to have fairly sturdy but mobile players.

What about the names I've left out?

Now to the nitty gritty. Yes, there are an awful lot of people not in the Will Carling Dream Team. I had so many people to consider, all of them great players. So there just had to be some notable omissions – all sorts of famous names who have not got in the side.

I can't begin to tell you all how difficult every choice was. There was so much scrubbing out and pencilling back in. I could almost have drawn up my Dream Team from the scraps of paper left on the floor.

My team has ended up without Wade Dooley. Brian Moore's not in, nor is Bill Beaumont. Jeff Probyn, one of the best scrummagers of all time, has had to be dropped off my over-long list. You only have to think of all the talent that England have had, in the back row especially. I could have played Roger Uttley, Peter Dixon, Ben Clarke, Tim Rodber, Micky Skinner and Mike Teague.

They're all great players. I just hope I have lost no notable friends. Mike Teague may say he will never talk to me again – but I hope he'll understand!

But perhaps the biggest surprise of all will be the omission of Rob Andrew, whose Number Ten shirt I've given to Richard Sharp. With Number Ten you are just spoilt for choice. Obviously Rob is a great player. But Sharp was a great runner, and I believed an out-and-out runner was what was required in this team.

I'm not saying Rob can't do it. But if I placed him in the Number Ten shirt people would accuse me of being biased and I would hate that.

WILL CARLING'S DREAM TEAM

There are so many people out there whom I have had to consider ... and sadly some of the all-time favourites have had to be dropped in favour of other players who were need to create a more rounded, winning team.

Aren't some members of my Dream Team a very personal choice?

Yes, I have to admit it. Some of my team choices were influenced by my own heroes from the past, as well as my present-day ones. Like all schoolboys, I had my favourites. David Duckham was one of them. He was fast and had great balance. One of my early, vivid memories of him was when he was actually playing in the 1973 Barbarians game against New Zealand. I thought Duckham was just outstanding. I also remember him scoring a try against the French in Paris. I just think he had a great side-step, yet had the courage to run as well. He really used to take people on. He's quite a big man and was a truly great player.

Sure, Duckham was one of my heroes. But we've still got great people like Nigel Melville, Fran Cotton and Peter Wheeler – scorers from the 1980 Grand Slam.

Are some of the Fifteen linked to particular games?

Yes – one would always associate Duckham with the '73 Barbarians. And Richard Sharp with the great match against Scotland in 1963.

When you consider the forwards, it's usually harder to remember them for certain games. The bits that stick in my mind are Peter Winterbottom's first international against France when he hit Jean-Pierre Rieves at the tail of a lineout, and Paul Ackford because the first game he played was also my first game as captain. Three years later, people were saying he was the best lineout jumper in the world, which is why I picked him.

Then there were the highlights of players' careers. Someone like Jeremy Guscott in the '93 Lions Tour who played as well as I've ever seen a centre play. He was unbelievable, he really was. People now say he's not back to that form, but I think he is. I think it's still there. It's up to everyone else to give him the opportunity.

Mike Catt is another player with huge potential. The try he set up for Tony Underwood against France in 1995 was brilliant. He's got some great touches, and will go on to be one of the great players.

So we have our Fifteen, all of whom in their own way are very talented

But how on earth is this lot going to knit together as a team?

The honest answer is: you can never tell. However, just take a look at the back row – they would all know each other from around the same time. Take Peter Winterbottom, for whom I have huge respect, and Jon Hall as he was before his knee injuries in '87.

They would be a truly dynamic duo – they'd knit extremely well. Winterbottom said Hall was the most gifted athlete he had ever played with. Playing in his famed form, he's an explosive player.

People may tell me that Tony Neary should have been the Number Seven, but I'm biased because I just think Winterbottom is probably the hardest player I have ever played with – one of the great attitudes, just incredible.

And there's Dean Richards, just to hold it all together. He's fitter than he's ever been. I think you can afford to have him at Number Eight when you also have Martin Johnson, who is very athletic. So is Ackford – he'd be very mobile.

The tight five looks really good. You've got the strength of Fran Cotton and Jason Leonard and Peter Wheeler. I don't think you'll get them pushed around. They're a trio who'll go all right. The back is a bit more unpredictable but, no, I think it will be a fairly awesome team.

How about positional strengths?

I can't find many weaknesses there. Just look at the various abilities they've got. The Dream Team has a good scrummaging outfit and a very good lineout presence. You could have Jon Hall, who is there as jumper – so suddenly you have the presence of three good jumpers, three world class jumpers. It's a very strong front row.

Then you have good tackling strength at half back, as well as the ability to move the ball. With those kind of runners and flair, you can attack from anywhere.

Which areas of the pitch will be most crucial to my Dream Team being a success?

Most of the game gets played between the two ten-yard lines. So the point of the game is how you play from there. It's whether you have the confidence to move into the midfield or whether you use the likes of David Duckham and Rory Underwood – because Rory, although not big, is explosively one of the strongest people around.

The side I have picked would use the ball in the hand more between the two ten-yard lines. It's the same with the scrum – which I believe will have the ability to move the ball quickly into the midfield. That, by the way, is where Southern Hemisphere sides are very good. They move the ball quickly, they get to the breakdown and then develop into a broken field situation. I think what I've got is a very good broken field side. That's where it's at its strongest.

What would be my team tactics if I were sending them out?

For a start, I'd hope that everyone else would be too afraid to play them! You are talking about world class set pieces, so you have got to concentrate on the basics first – scrummaging and lineouts – making sure that they get those off pat. Then you must actually get involved around the field. I would like to see the ball in hand an awful lot with those kind of backs. But you never neglect kicking – you use that as a tactic, which they would put to good effect.

I have a good back row to make sure they play quite a continuous game. I would then bring Jason Leonard and Fran Cotton into the game to play ball-in-hand a great deal. And I have very dynamic backs. I mean, how you defend with the likes of Duckham, Rory, Catt and Co coming at you?

I am very happy with the team as a strategic entity. There's huge pace there.

Is my famous Fifteen a winning team – or just an entertaining one?

It's no use having a team that sets out to entertain if it doesn't also aim to win at all costs.

My theory is always that, first and foremost, you have to WIN. People want you to win, they really do. If you can win and entertain, that's a bonus. Having said which, everyone likes to watch a win with STYLE. What I have to remember, however, is that my Dream Team is not a Barbarian side, it's an England side. So we've got to win.

But what about me?

I bet you're wondering: Wouldn't he like to be in the team himself. Or to captain it? Or to coach it?

Hope you won't be disappointed … but I reckon my best role in the Dream Team would be outside it. By choice, I would be a non-playing captain

If anyone asked me, that is!

MIKE CATT

The first position – full back – in my all time greatest side goes to my team mate Mike Catt. Mike was an obvious choice, despite his recent forays into the Number Ten shirt. He's not been around for long, but he's a brilliant footballer – more than an out-and-out full back. He has great touch.

He's a fine kicker and has real pace. He makes some great lines when he links with the three-quarters.

One of Mike's major strengths is that when he's in a hole and he knows he's not going to make it, he has the ability to change direction and look for support.

INTERNATIONAL DEBUT:
VS. WALES 1994

CAPS:
13

POSITION:
FULL BACK

Very few players can do that. It's hard for anyone, because your instinct is to carry on running as fast as you can. But that's what Mike did when he set up Tony Underwood's try against France.

Mike knows that, defensively, he's very good. I just think he has something different.

His confidence gives him that extra edge. He's going to make a huge difference to England this year. And like so many players from South Africa, he has the attitude of wanting to play running rugby at all costs.

So Mike's in because I believe him to be courageous, full of confidence and a born winner.

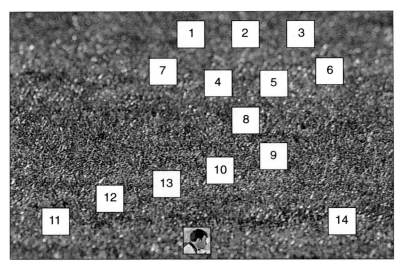

In a game which has rocketed from obscurity to world prominence in the Nineties, Mike Catt's meteoric rise to fame has more than anyone else personified the amazing rise of the sport and its players. Just a couple of years ago, if you had stopped to pick up a paper at a Bath newsagent, it is just possible that the 'till boy' – his own expression – was a personable young South African wearing a dark blue smock.

My, how things have changed! Now you could walk into any newsagents in the land and chances are you will see the brilliant England full back smiling out of one of those papers.

Catt arrived in the West Country for a holiday in 1993 and became England's first-choice full back. He had headed over here for a couple of months' holiday with an uncle in Stroud, Gloucestershire. He had played the game in Port Elizabeth, South Africa, so he thought he'd try a few phone calls to see if he could get on field, have somebody to appraise his skills and maybe get a game somewhere.

For a long time, he got nowhere. The telephone stayed silent. Then finally it rang. It was Gareth Chilcott, the Bath coach whom all aficionados will recall as being one of the greatest prop forwards ever to play for Bath and England. Mike, he said, should show up at the Recreation Ground, Bath's home, and try out at a training session.

The rest as they say, is history. His rise to fame makes Roy of the Rovers pale into insignificance. His aggressive, hard running, hard hitting talent is typical of the South African game and he was the talk of the town's rugby cognoscenti from that very first session.

Yet luck has been on his side. Who would have foretold that Jeremy Guscott, his illustrious team-mate to be, would suffer a groin injury that would put him out of the game for months? Or the surprise retirement of Stuart Barnes, another Bath and England star? Or that Paul Hull, England's regular full-back, voted the national side's man of the tour when he returned from a series against South Africa last year, would suffer an Achilles' tendon strain in a game against Canada at Twickenham, thus giving Catt the chance to score two brilliant tries?

England coach Jack Rowell kept Mike on as a first team starter for the Five Nations Championship – to the fury it must be said, of the 'Twickers' cadre of Pressmen who pointed to his lack of experience as a full-back. His career had been spent as a fly half. 'He probably knows more about surfing,' the pundits said.

18

Yet Rowell had the last word at the end of the season. 'He has been superb, hasn't he?' he asked. And no-one could deny it.

Catt is still more than a little bewildered at the speed with which everything has happened. He said: 'I was 21 when I came over and was paying £380 a month for a one-bedroomed flat. I didn't know a soul. Didn't know how to work the central heating. Didn't have a telephone. Didn't have a clue. I was just a little lost South African boy, I suppose.

'I'd be back in South Africa now if it hadn't been for that job selling newspapers. I have Malcolm Pearce of Johnson's to thank for that. He is a big Bath rugby fan and was my boss then. I'm not a till boy anymore. I've risen up to be more of a public relations man for Malcolm's company.'

Latterly, Catt has become one of the leading professional players in the land, quitting his job as a marketing executive to become virtually the first full-time pro in the country. He will get £40,000 a year as an England international, and will supplement that lucratively with marketing and promotion and possibly TV and newspaper work.

The big question he always gets asked is: would you rather be playing full-back for World Champions South Africa? He is always adamant he would not.

'England has given me my big break,' he says, and points out that his roots are wholly English, even if he is a little shaky about where they were planted. 'My grandparents came from Kent, or was it Surrey,' he says. 'Anyway, from somewhere around those places. And my mother came back here for 10 years and married an Englishman before she went back to South Africa. My two elder brothers were born in Aylesbury; myself and my younger brother in South Africa.

He understands the Afrikaaner tongue, though, and he still laughs about the massive embarrassment caused at a reception when he relayed some of the not-so-pretty local remarks about England to the English side. 'They had no idea I could understand the language,' he laughs. 'I love Bath, though. The locals are so easy going. It is such a beautiful place and, no, the weather doesn't bother me, although it does my girlfriend Debbie. Just now and then I might think of where my brothers live in the Eastern Cape Province, in St Francis Bay with a boat in the marina there, surfing at the weekend. The atmosphere is so much more relaxed there now. I'm not political but when I went back there recently it was brilliant to see black and white mingling.

'But, no. It is pointless of me to be thinking of going back there in the foreseeable future. I have become part of the Bath family.

There was a slight hiccup in the 'Roy of the Rovers' story when England was hammered in the World Cup semi by New Zealand. As Ian Stirrup wrote in the Daily Star: 'Catt made a lasting impression on the Newlands turf – where Jonah Lomu trampled him into the ground scoring one of his tries!'

DAVID DUCKHAM

At Number Fourteen, I have chosen a truly great player. David Duckham once told me that he envied Tony Underwood and the other players who have worn this shirt in more recent times.

For me, however, the Number Fourteen IS David Duckham himself.

I grew up watching Duckham and had the chance to play with him. I marvelled at his balance. He was the master of the body swerve and deft side step. He was a big man but he was very graceful, and at his best he was uncatchable. Whether it was for England or during his days as captain of Coventry, his graceful running was a beautiful sight.

Duckham inspired a generation of would-be rugby internationals – myself included particularly as Duckham, too, is an old Sedberghian – and was one of the most imitated players on school grounds around the country. David never had the chance to play in a really great England side, which made his achieve-

INTERNATIONAL DEBUT:
VS. IRELAND 1969

CAPS:
38

POSITION:
RIGHT WING

ments all the more admirable. He still shone many times.

He once told me when we were having a chat in South Africa that he would have given anything to have played in the present-day set-up – not because of the players who were around with him at the time, but because of the success he could have achieved.

He had worked out that they won less than 25 per cent of the games in which he played, and we as an England team now win 75 per cent to 80 per cent of the games we play. Dave said he found that very demoralising for a guy of his talent.

I don't think it was ever a reflection on the state of English rugby. We just did not see the best of an awful lot of the players who were around in that era.

Dave, however, managed to show his own brand of brilliance. But if he'd thought he was playing in a winning team, you'd have seen a lot more of him – particularly with his flowing b l o n d locks!

If you'd had David around now, he would be unbelievable. A modern English side which included David Duckham would be impossible to beat.

21

David Duckham, born in Coventry in 1946, played 38 times for England between 1969-76 and scored 10 tries. But that harvest is scant reward for a winger who had it all – the strength and power of a big man and the skill and speed of a whippet.

Duckham, who played for both Coventry and Warwickshire was unfortunate to be in an English back line riddled by safety-first instincts instead of adventure. So it was all too rarely that he was given the opportunity to display those flowing skills. It still did not prevent him being the most feared Englishman of his day in the Five Nations Championship. And David Duckham was also good enough to force his way into the British Lions Test team in New Zealand in 1971.

Even the star-studded Welsh team, in those days the supreme force in the northern hemisphere, harboured tremendous respect for the big, blond power-house. Indeed, he was christened 'Dai Duckham' by the Welsh, an accolade never previously bestowed on any Englishman! And Gerald Davies` still recalls David Duckham as the most difficult opponent he ever had to face. 'He had this

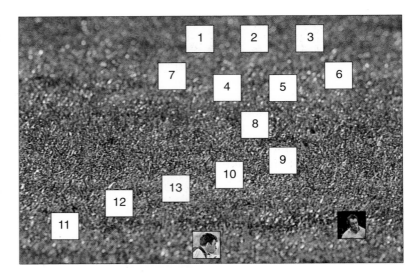

great big arse which he would stick out, making him almost impossible to tackle,' says Davies.

Duckham had a feverish enthusiasm for the game. He used to demand early ball, to give him the space and time to break into full, raking stride. His pleadings too often went unanswered, however. Perhaps Duckham was making his own subtle point when he once wrote that, 'English back play has always been associated with forthrightness, physical presence and no little valour.'

No mention of adventure there. And that was a sad epitaph to a truly outstanding player.

JEREMY GUSCOTT

What greater sacrifice can any captain make than to give up his Number Thirteen shirt to a colleague!

But in my place I have chosen Jeremy Guscott – because, quite simply, Jeremy is one of the most skilful people I have ever played with.

I've played more than 30 tests with him and never ceased to be amazed at how effortlessly he coasts past opponents with silky speed. He gives the appearance of not being a fast mover when in reality he has to be one of the quickest players around today.

You don't think he's going that fast and then he's gone! He's just so smooth. There appears to be no effort there when he runs. He just passes people!

He is always very aware, and I often think he must have his own personal radar system – a 360 degree radar!

I just think he's got something different –

INTERNATIONAL DEBUT:
VS. RUMANIA 1989

CAPS:
40

POSITION:
CENTRE

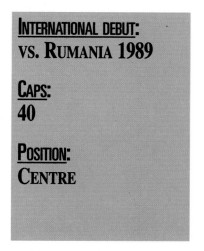

and I am not the only person to think so. When you play against him, you want to ask him his secrets … more so than when you play with him!

I think he's still got it, even though people say he's maybe not the same since his injury. I don't agree. I think it's up to him to bring that talent back out again and I think he will. He's a great player.

I also think people's expectations of him since he came back are huge. They expect him to cut sides open. You don't do that any more – or at least very rarely.

Jeremy managed it during that one, inspirational run in the World Cup, when he opened Scotland up twice and actually managed to get a try. But it's very hard to do that with so many forwards waiting to stop you in your tracks.

One of the great things Guscott does (which people don't seem to understand) is to create space, because people worry about him. And as they mark him, he creates space for other people. That is a very underestimated attribute.

No one else on our side could have done what Jeremy has done. He still has tremendous gifts and it's up to us to bring them out. People also wrongly say that he's not great defensively. But I've got to tell you … he's one of the best !

Jeremy, quite simply, is one of the most gifted people I have ever played with.

23

Jeremy Guscott is one of those supreme beings you find just once in a generation – a gifted athlete who plays every game with great panache. As a child, he was West of England judo champion in his weight category and competed in the national championships. He is a brilliant golfer, a good cricketer and had trials for both Bristol City and Rovers. But, from an early age, he told everyone who cared to listen that one day he would play rugby for Bath and England.

His friend and England team-mate Rob Andrew wrote: 'How often have I longed for the self-confidence which oozes from Jeremy Guscott's every pore whenever he takes the field. It is the ability to erase the most calamitous error from one's mind in the almost certain knowledge that some time, somewhere along the line there will be a touch of match-winning genius.'

Sometimes those qualities which make an athlete outstanding can produce a tiresome personality. If you read some of the profiles written about him, you might come to the conclusion that Guscott was a gifted rugby player ... but a bit of a prat!

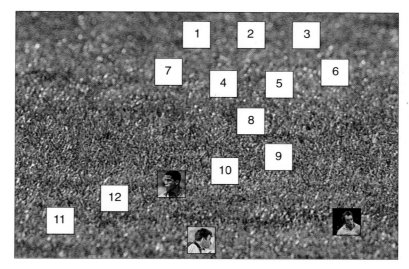

When approached by a girl for a dance he is alleged to have replied, 'Why? It isn't Halloween yet, is it?' He says he doesn't remember saying it. Another jibe was that he hadn't scored for Bath for so long because his head wouldn't fit between the posts. He smiles enduringly at the joke. Nothing could be further from the truth.

As rugby develops into the 21st century, it has shed, or is in the process of shedding, its middle class, public school image. Guscott, more than anybody, portrays the new image. He was even dubbed 'Guzza' by one tabloid newspaper – a rare accolade in the sport. Jeremy was expelled from his school, and in his own words, spent most of his teens 'dossing around and playing video machines' until rugby sorted him out.

'I don't think about it these days,' he says. 'I don't like looking back. Rugby sorted me out. Gareth Chilcott was a tremendous influence. He taught me how to be part of a team. The strength of Bath is that none of the players wants to be the one who lets the side down.'

It was team-mate David Trick who read him the main sermon. Guscott cadged a lift in Trick's car and asked him if the other players thought he was arrogant. Trick told him they did. Trick recalls, 'I told him that you have to have some arrogance, but that he had too much. I told him he was a great player but a prat.' Guscott took the hint.

His normal flair game has suffered in recent seasons, as the sport as a whole has become bogged down with set pieces and power games. England have become Northern hemisphere experts at it. Guscott says: 'There have been the Grand Slams and the World Cups and the tremendous experience of playing for your country. There have been big rewards. But the old joy in simply playing the game has declined quite sharply.

'I am as streetwise as any player, and not one to shirk the dirty jobs on the field. But to me, my role should be more than running up and down the field chasing kicks, making and missing tackles. It should be about running with the ball in your hands, and if a centre, any centre, is not doing that any more then something must have gone wrong.

'Perhaps the English are too conservative by nature. I spoke to Aussie centre Jason Little after the World Cup and he said England have the best three-quarter line in the world but hardly ever used it. Rob Andrew has tremendous value to the England side in many departments. But he is difficult for centres to play with, not being naturally quick off the mark. He does not have the ideal style for launching back play at pace.'

Guscott is much more suited by having Stuart Barnes at fly- half. In 1993, Guzza was an automatic selection for the Lions, along with partner Carling, after another top notch season in which he claimed five-point tries against Canada, South Africa and Scotland, and dropped a rare goal in the defeat by Wales at Cardiff.

For many though, his most memorable contribution of the campaign was his part in the wonderful move which led to Rory Underwood's try against the Scots. Barnes's break and divine pass allowed Jerry to stretch his legs like the thoroughbred he is, leave the Scottish defence for dead and then release Underwood.

On a domestic note, Guscott is still helping Bath to titles, despite last year's aberration. He started his career with their mini-section as a wing, aged seven. His meteoric rise in 1989 brought two England B caps, three tries on his full England debut against Rumania in Bucharest, and one invitation from the British Lions – before he was capped by England.

His reported best moment in the game came in the Second Test in Brisbane, where he scored a marvellous and crucial try to give the Lions a 19-12 win, which brought them back into a series they eventually won. He was ever-present in England's back-to-back Grand Slams and wore the Number 12 jersey in the 1991 World Cup final defeat by the Aussies. He also toured New Zealand with a World XV in 1992, playing in their first Test defeat of the All Blacks.

Could he be lured into rugby league? 'No way,' he says. 'I've had the offers but I have always been more attracted to the game in Australia than England.' The most recent offer was £200,000 a year to play for Bradford in the Super League.

But when Guscott looks to the future, he doesn't want to become a full-time professional player. He is happy combining his careers at Bath and the Gas Board. When he contemplates retirement, he sees a job in broadcasting as the ideal possibility.

CLIVE WOODWARD

At Number Twelve, I have selected Clive Woodward. The word 'elusive' springs to mind when I think of Clive in full flow, and he has often been compared to the great Barry John – with good reason. It wasn't the size of him – he just had the ability to move. That immediately gives him a very important role in this team.

Clive has that enviable skill of being able to create space for other players. He is one of the most creative centres England have ever produced. And he has brilliant balance.

But what attracted me to Clive was that he had the confidence to run at people. I remember watching him run through a seemingly impenetrable mass of opponents – again, moving a bit like Barry John.

INTERNATIONAL DEBUT:
VS. IRELAND 1980

CAPS:
21

POSITION:
CENTRE

But it is not just about speed. Clive possesses the guile actually to beat players … and for me that is what rugby is all about.

Clive Woodward exploded onto the England scene in 1980, coinciding, happily, with the Bill Beaumont-inspired revolution which changed the face of English rugby.

Woodward was one of the great side-steppers of the game, but on top of this he was, above everything else, a team man who created openings and space for his team-mates.

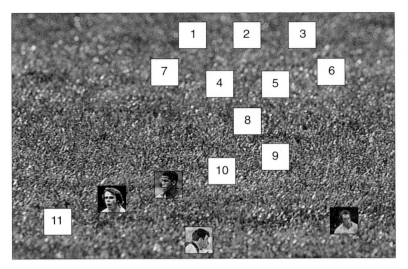

Woodward made his debut against Ireland in the 1980 Grand Slam outfit. Such was his impact that he also made the Lions tour of South Africa the same year.

He played with massive influence for Harlequins and Leicester. Beaumont, never one to lavish praise on contemporaries, has him marked down as his best ever centre. 'He had not only speed, but guile,' smiles Bill. 'But above everything else, he was a beautifully balanced runner. He ran at opponents, then just when you thought he was sure to be downed, he produced a breathtaking sidestep and left his man for dead.'

His England career did not last as long as it should. He was in the British Lions party which toured New Zealand in 1983, but never made the Test side and a year later he won the last of his 21 caps. He did, however, establish a reputation few players have equalled. His ability to run through a seemingly impenetrable mass of players and emerge still clutching the ball has rarely been equalled.

After years of boring rugby, dominated by Wales and the All Blacks, England was suddenly transformed into a side to be reckoned with. And that has to be put down to Beaumont's magnificent powers of leadership and the thrilling influence of great players like Woodward.

But Woodward's influence on the English game did not stop there in 1984. He moved to Australia and made a big name for himself playing for the New South Wales side Manley. One of his recruits whilst there was a young fly-half whose potential Woodward spotted instantly. His name? Rob Andrew.

Andrew says fondly of Woodward: 'I will never forget the advice and encouragement Clive passed on. He taught me a lot about the game and I am a big fan. He was a totally unselfish player who made others around him look good. There is a lot of the Will Carling in him, and I am not surprised Will chose him at right centre in his Dream Team.'

Carling himself adds: 'It is not just about speed, it is about guile. And Clive always had the guile to beat players and that for me is what rugby is all about.'

29

RORY UNDERWOOD

Next, I have picked one of the all-time best try scorers. Rory Underwood wins my vote at Number Eleven. He's one of the most explosive players I have witnessed and just having him in your side puts the fear of God into your opposition!

Rory has developed his game and he has improved his kicking greatly in recent years. That's a huge part of the wingers' armoury.

There is something the Southern Hemisphere has taught us – and that is the long ball game. If you are going to play it, you've got to have people at the back who can kick huge distances. And Rory has worked very hard on that.

He did a lot of work with the bobsleigh team with the Olympic squad, which has helped him become one of the most explosive people you could come across, power for power. Not only is he fast, but he's incredibly powerful. And very hard to stop.

Some of the tries he has scored have been staggering. Like many of my

INTERNATIONAL DEBUT:
VS. IRELAND 1984

CAPS:
79

POSITION:
LEFT WING

Dream Team, Rory is above all a THREAT! You know that if you have him hanging around out there on the pitch, people will get worried about him. He goes on his experience and nothing else. He's very fast off the mark and finishes. He's a great finisher.

This was the overriding

factor when I sat down to choose this team. It just has to be a winning side. Entertain by all means — but win! Rory Underwood is a winner.

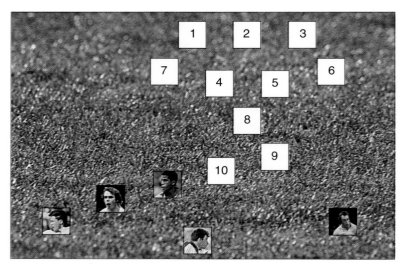

There are times when you could have forgiven the England rugby fan for abandoning the traditional 'Swing Low Sweet Chariot' anthem and singing instead 'Land of Hope and Rory'. The flying winger — and of course he's in the RAF too — has been the nation's hero for years.

Rory Underwood is our most successful wing and try scorer ever, clawing his way into the record books after something of a mid-career dip.

The winger has a dream and a nightmare. The dream is always of scoring the match-winning try in the corner, hurtling through the air at full stretch. And Rory has done plenty of that. When the dream comes off, it is undoubtedly the most thrilling sight in sport, and one of the bravest. It is the moment the crowd waits for, a ball zipped along the three-quarter line for the winger to set off on his dramatic dash to the line. It is the moment that crystallises all the power, beauty and courage the game has to offer. And one man does it more than most – Rory Underwood.

Underwood (born in Middlesbrough in 1963) has a younger brother who plays for England, and a Malaysian mother who made mincemeat out of Jonah Lomu in a television Pizza Hut advert! But no one can upstage Rory. He has become the ultimate hero, handsome, dashing, the nation's pin-up boy.

Cyril Lowe's aggregate record of 18 tries for England had stood unthreatened for 67 years. And, against the Irish a couple of years ago, there was an agonising 75 minutes when Rory rarely had a sniff of the ball. Five minutes from the end, however, the ball found its own way to him. It was only a half chance but, no matter, the race was on.

The Irish cover swarmed across the pitch and Underwood blazed onwards. Ten yards from the line, as the defence closed in, Underwood's dash seemed doomed. Then he took off. Crossan and Mullin lunged, but too late. Rory was in at the corner; try number 19 was on the scoreboard and 'Rory, Rory Hallelujah' was in the record books.

That try was a cameo of self-assurance. Underwood carried conviction in every stride. Legendary French centre Jo Maso says: 'From the moment he gets the ball he has only one idea in his head, and that is to score.'

His success has run parallel with England's. Now 32, Rory's first 23 caps were spent in virtual solitary confinement, marooned on the wing watching a side stuttering through each international season. From his cocoon on the wing,

Underwood managed only four tries.

'I was just turning out for England in those days,' Underwood humbly confesses. 'It sounds terrible, but although I was very proud to play for my country I did not have a lot of enthusiasm about the general set-up. I just drifted along with things, and I think it showed in my play. I lacked real drive and purpose.'

Times have changed. England has changed and so has Underwood. By 1991, Rory had broken David Duckham's record of 36 caps and had become a player of immense potency. He is widely regarded as being the best winger in the game today.

A distant glimpse of the line is all it takes for the Underwood muscles to twitch expectantly and for crowds all over the world to strain forward eagerly.

Even his defence, which was probably his weakest point, has improved beyond all recognition. Underwood still refuses to watch video footage of his most infamous clanger, however, when he allowed Ieuan Evans to sneak up on him at Cardiff Arms Park in 1989. He was the only person among the 70,000 witnesses who didn't see Evans thundering up on him as Underwood tried to retrieve the ball near his own line. The result was Wales's only try … and a famous victory which wrecked England's Grand Slam hopes. Rory sat for hours afterwards, utterly inconsolable in the dressing room.

Yet Underwood's defensive tackling nowadays is as good as anyone will find, Jonah Lomu not withstanding. Underwood has always had ability and physical prowess. Tom McNab, fitness adviser to the England squad until recently, and former AAA coach, says of him: 'He has the finest natural physique I've ever come across.' Among those McNab has come across include decathlon double gold medalist Daley Thomson. McNab reckons that Rory, given the right conditioning, could dent Daley's massive ego in one or two events.

Underwood though, was not born with that sort of ego – the bloated sense of self-supremacy which is the spur to every great champion. Underwood has not emerged from the shadows by some miracle implant of egomania. He is as modest and self-effacing as he ever was. What he has learned is to react more positively to others around him, to get himself into a game even when the game refuses to come to him.

The change really came with the arrival of Geoff Cooke and the new England/Carling set-up. Underwood responded to the new streamlined intensive structure.

The first warnings came in 1988 when England thrashed the living daylights out of Ireland. They went into the match, the last of that year's Five Nations games, without a try to their names. By the end of it, they had six, more than they had achieved in four previous championships! Rory scored twice, and his personal roll was on.

'That was the first sign of things to come,' he says. 'Gradually we all began to play with more confidence and conviction. There was also far more continuity under Cooke. I didn't train any differently. I didn't spend hours practising the dive for the corner. But I do approach games, training and international get-togethers in a much more positive frame of mind. If the side plays well, the wingers usually do.'

RICHARD SHARP

One of my most surprising choices to many England fans will be the man who wears the Number Ten shirt.

I have risked Rob Andrew never buying me a drink again... I have also reluctantly overlooked Stuart Barnes. Instead, I have awarded the shirt to a man who made his debut before I was even born. My half back

INTERNATIONAL DEBUT:
VS. WALES 1960

CAPS:
14

POSITION:
FLY HALF

is Richard Sharp.

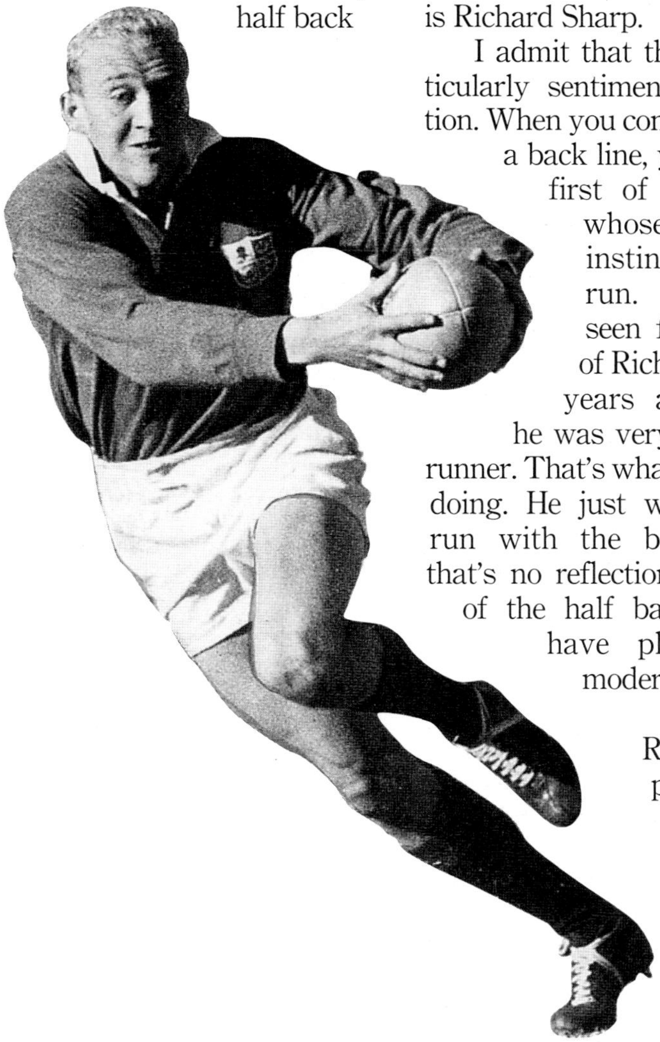

I admit that this a particularly sentimental selection. When you come to pick a back line, you think first of someone whose first instinct is to run. I have seen film clips of Richard from years ago, and he was very much a runner. That's what he liked doing. He just wanted to run with the ball. And that's no reflection on any of the half backs who have played in modern times.

When Richard played in

the 1960s, it may have been easier to be a runner. Today the game is different. But I still think he would have the mentality to cope with the modern game.

Sharp is a very talented man, and would shake up any team and bring out the best in everyone else. He's a controversial choice, maybe even a risky one — but one that I think my team will definitely get away with.

35

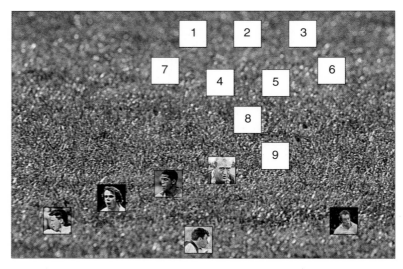

Richard Sharp burst onto the international scene with such devastating impact back in 1960 that he was christened the 'Redruth Diamond'. What most people didn't realise was that this particular gem was mined in Mysore, India. That's where Sharp was born, in 1938, the son of Cornish mining engineer who was working on a long-term contract in the sub-continent.

Sharp was seven years old when the family returned to England. But the game was already in his blood. His rugby-mad dad, Fred, had made him an honorary member of Wasps at birth! It was in Cornwall that the family settled, however, and in the West Country where schoolboy Richard displayed his exceptional sporting talent, captaining his school's rugby and cricket teams.

Rugby was his abiding passion, though, and Sharp first came to national prominence when he won his blue at Oxford. He was still at university when he was named one of England's reserves for the start of the 1959-60 campaign against Wales at Twickenham. Fate played its fickle hand when Bev

Risman, the first-choice outside half, pulled out with injury less than 24 hours before kick-off. That let Sharp in – and his brilliant, elusive running destroyed a Welsh team which had been champions the previous season.

Sharp kept his place all season, performing the starring role as England, against all expectations, won the championship. The following season he scored one of the greatest tries ever witnessed at Twickenham, his quicksilver burst from 25 yards leaving a host of Scottish defenders clutching air. He toured South Africa with the British Lions in 1962, only to have his summer ruined by a vicious Springbok tackle which broke his cheekbone. Three

years later, at the age of 27, he stunned the rugby world by announcing his retirement.

Sharp had won 13 caps and captured his own place in sporting folklore. Sadly, he was persuaded to step back to England's aid two years later when he was only a pale shadow of his former self, as his side was crushed 23-11 by Australia. But that sad final bow should not disguise his earlier greatness. Not since the halcyon days of Prince Obolensky, had England had such a regal figure at their helm.

NIGEL MELVILLE

The Number Nine shirt goes to one of my predecessors as England captain: Nigel Melville. With apologies to Dewi Morris and the others, I believe Nigel is the most talented scrum half in the modern history of the game – a player who really did have everything.

Nigel captained England on his international debut and was skipper for a couple of games when I was in the team. He was very fast and very talented. He had a great strategic brain, could run like the wind, and he had a great pass… I mean a really great pass!

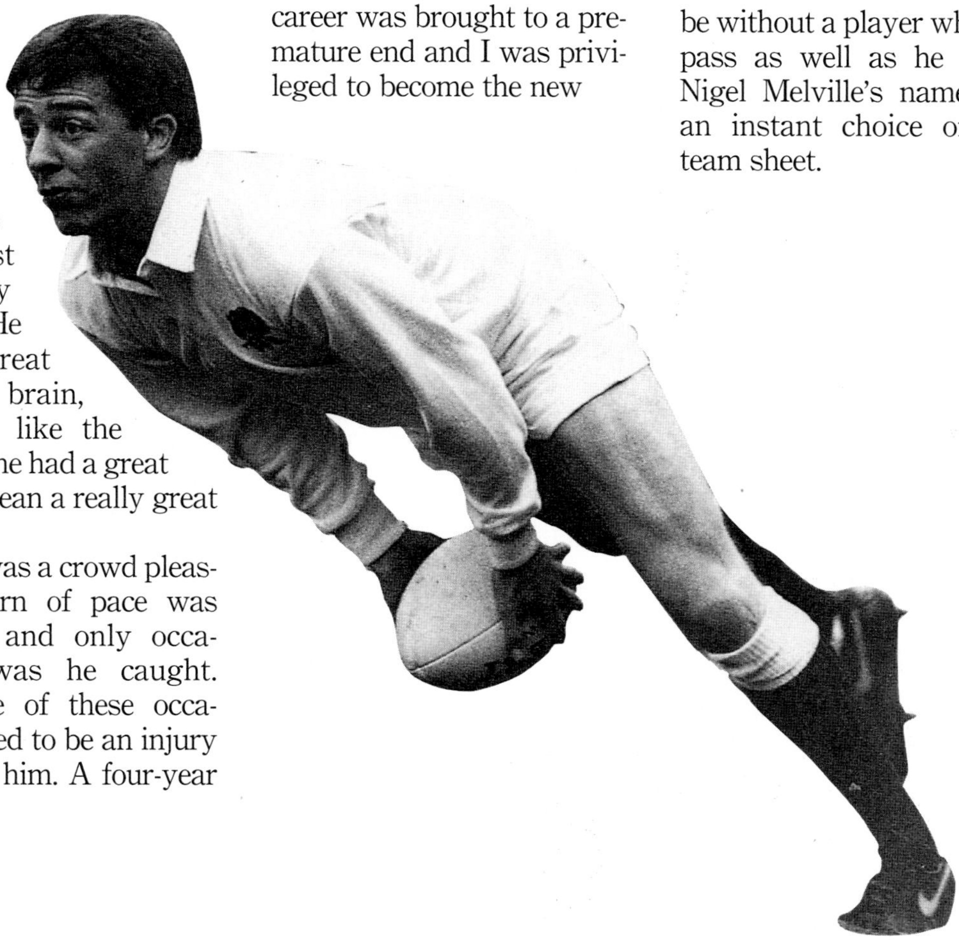

Nigel was a crowd pleaser. His turn of pace was explosive and only occasionally was he caught. Sadly, one of these occasions proved to be an injury too far for him. A four-year

INTERNATIONAL DEBUT:
VS. AUSTRALIA 1984

CAPS:
13

POSITION:
SCRUM HALF

career was brought to a premature end and I was privileged to become the new

England captain shortly afterwards.

If my side is to play the rugby I want it to play, it must have someone like Nigel to provide service from the base of the scrum. It's a great shame that injury so hampered his career. He would have been there for many, many years if he had not suffered the injuries he did.

But no side can afford to be without a player who can pass as well as he could. Nigel Melville's name was an instant choice on my team sheet.

Nigel Melville ended a British Lions tour of New Zealand in a neck-brace. The merciless All Blacks had marked him a potential danger man. A knee aimed viciously at his head put paid to that. Sadly, that vivid picture cameos Nigel's whole career – for the Wasps scrum half had become a casualty department on two legs by the time he was finally forced to hang up his boots in 1988.

Melville had the heart of a giant, the speed of a cobra and a handling and passing ability never seen before or since at the base of England's scrum. But in the fierce arena of international rugby, those qualities made him a high-priority target for opposing forwards. He was hit hard and often. And those injuries, and in particular those battered, ravaged knees, could simply not take the strain.

Born in 1961, Melville had already established his international place by the age of 22. It did not take long to prove his leadership qualities to the selectors, who gave him the captain's role. But that chronic catalogue of injuries limited his international appearances to just 13 – a tragic waste of a glorious talent.

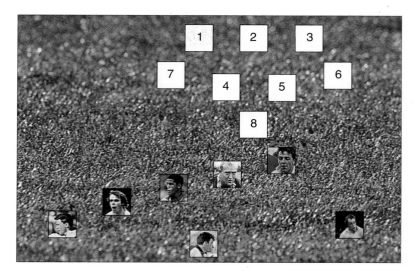

Ironically, if his body had been able to absorb the physical battering, Will Carling might never have become England's most successful captain. It was Carling, then a thrusting young centre, who was named to assume the mantle when Melville bowed out. Within two years, the England team won the Grand Slam. A year after that, England reached the World Cup final, losing to Australia.

Melville was only 30 at that time. He would surely have still been the scrum half and inspiration if he had been fit. And who knows? With his guiding genius, England might just have turned glorious World Cup final failure into wondrous triumph!

DEAN RICHARDS

Dean Richards is vastly underestimated. He is a great ball handler and a great focus for a side. In sport, the buzzword 'Focus' has become a cliche, but in Dean I have a Number Eight who knows exactly what he wants to achieve. He's a really hard competitor, with a great determination to win.

Dean has to be one of the most self-confident men I know. He's almost arrogant — but also almost a saint! There are players who do an awful lot of the hard work on the field yet are so quiet that they never say anything about it. Dean is one of those. He has a mental strength that he can actually pass on to other people.

My team would be trying to play quite a fast game. Every now and again it's going to slow up, however, and that's where Dean would come into his own. He manages to turn up at the right time in the right space when

INTERNATIONAL DEBUT:
VS. IRELAND 1986

CAPS:
48

POSITION:
NUMBER EIGHT

you least expect him. He's not conventional, by any means. I admit that there are some things he doesn't do, because he runs different lines from most of the rest of the team. But he makes up for it in other areas. He plays his own game and 90 per cent of the time it comes off.

Dean has such a drive to win that I sometimes have to try to persuade him to free up the ball quickly — but I don't have a problem with that. He is a truly great player, a tough competitor who has mental as well as physical strength. I believe that in him I have the best possible choice for the Number Eight shirt.

41

Imagine a bulldog chewing a wasp. Imagine a man with the most ungainly walk in rugby history. Imagine the one man you would not pick a fight with in a bar ... and you have Dean Richards.

In a world of hard cases, 'Deano' is the one you would want on your side. He is one of the most unorthodox and commanding figures in world rugby.

Richards missed the whole of England's 1990 programme with a serious shoulder injury. But not half as much as England missed him. His return to the England fold was crucial in the battle of the mind. England, Carling's England, had thrown body and soul into their unsuccessful attempt on the Grand Slam the previous season, and it would have been easy for the England squad subconsciously to have thrown in the towel – to have lost impetus because of the looming possibility that they had done as much as they could ever have done and still fallen short.

The return of Richards changed all that. He was the new factor, the new strength. Richards was the proof that the team could still improve, that if they could put in another season

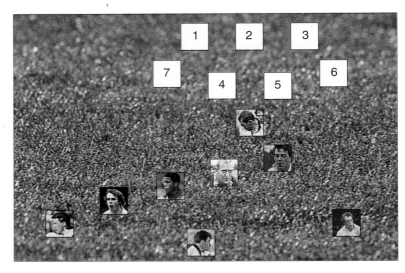

of dedication they would win through.

Dean Richards, born in Nuneaton, Warwickshire, in 1963, and who currently plays for Leicester, is quite simply the most remarkable Number Eight the world has seen. He is by no means a player of burning pace. He is not quite as dedicated a trainer as most in the England squad, and you would never read of his style in a rugby textbook. Nor is he a top line-out force. Yet his towering performances in the rose-patterned shirt belie all the down-sides.

He is his own man. His sheer power is remarkable. He has the particular talent of staying afloat and in control when clearing up the loose ball under the most severe pressure.

Time and again he has baled out his country by standing four square under pressure, protecting the ball and allowing his forwards to regroup around him. His locking up of possession is a feature of English play which has enabled the national squad to dominate the Northern Hemisphere.

The England back row of late has been dominant. But the game which stays in the imagination is his return against the Irish in Dublin. In a classic act, he wrenched the ball clear when an England movement was floundering dangerously in midfield, kept the move alive and heading upfield, and gave Rory Underwood the space to carve his way over for the critical try.

PETER WINTERBOTTOM

Peter Winterbottom very adequately fills the Number Seven shirt. He is the hardest player I have ever gone on to the field with. For that reason alone he wins a cap in the Will Carling Dream Team.

Many would have picked Tony Neary, and I could not dispute that. But, for me, Peter Winterbottom was always the biggest hitter. If he hit you, you knew about … you really did!

When I think of Peter, I immediately recall his first international when he hit Jean-Pierre Rieves at the tail of a lineout. That is one of the reasons I could not envisage fielding a team without him.

The way Peter picked up lines on people was often unnerving. He wasn't the fastest player, by any means, but he would always pick the best line and would always get there before the other guy to seize the ball.

He was a brilliant distributor of the ball but his main strength was always

INTERNATIONAL DEBUT:
VS. AUSTRALIA 1982

CAPS:
58

POSITION:
OPEN-SIDE FLANKER

his defence.

We played a good few tests together and had quite an understanding. Somehow you just knew where he was coming from, all the time. He was never a selfish or greedy player.

Peter enjoyed a decade of great rugby and became England's most capped forward. He was absolutely outstanding by the time he'd finished. He was truly world class.

To many rugby lovers, Peter Winterbottom was Rocky, Rambo and Superman all rolled into one. A man with nerves of steel, supernatural powers and who loved nothing better than a good scrap.

If there were two men you would pick to stand either side of you in the trenches, Dean Richards would be one and 'Winters' certainly the other. The Harlequins legend fought for his country 58 times on the rugby killing fields in a record-breaking career.

But while England's most capped forward scared the living daylights out of fellow flankers on the field, he was the gentlest, most sensitive of men off it.

No one appreciated the wonder of 'Winters' more than Will Carling. When it comes to judging meat, muscle and menace among the rugby tough guys who have competed for the Number One spot, Carling has no doubts about should come out on tops. Peter the Great wins, biceps down!

When Winterbottom retired at the ripe old age of 33 after the British Lions tour to New Zealand, having won 58 caps and just as many opposition scalps in the mauls, it did not just

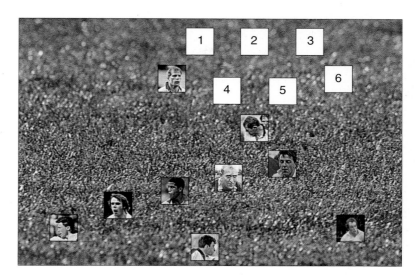

leave a gap for England to fill. It left a chasm.

Such was the respect that the then manager Geoff Cooke had for the Harlequins star that he asked him to help find the perfect replacement for the Number Seven jersey. Bath's Ben Clarke has tried his damnedest to fill that chasm. But Peter James Winterbottom MBE — 1991 and 1992 Grand Slam hero, and leader of Harlequins 1991 Pilkington Cup victory — was always going to be an impossible act to follow.

How Jack Rowell and friends could have done with some of the famed 'Winters' strong-armed stuff in South Africa during the summer of 1995. The Yorkshireman would have thoroughly relished the task

of stopping Jonah 'the juggernaut' Lomu in his stride.

A few months after he officially quit the game, Winterbottom was persuaded by Harlequins coach Bob Templeton to make a final cameo appearance against Newcastle in a Courage League game. In fact, when he answered the Quins injury SOS, he left the club's fans wishing he had kept going for a couple more years and not left too early.

Templeton's verdict, after Winterbottom had come on and shown the rest how to tackle following the half-time break, said it all: 'In that one half, he made more tackles than the rest of the side in the last three games. I wish I had eight forwards like him.'

Jack Rowell will, no doubt, echo that view.

JON HALL

It may surprise some, but the very first name to go down on my team sheet was that of Jon Hall. At Number Six, I have a man whom I had the real privilege to play with in 1990 and 1994. By then injury had taken its toll on him. But when you see film footage of him playing in the 1980s you remember what a great player he was in his heyday.

Many people might look at my team list and think: 'Oh God, Jon Hall.' But Peter Winterbottom, whom I admire as well as being a great friend, told me he thought Jon was the best back row man he'd ever played with.

I myself never played with Jon at his prime. But I recognise him to have been a very fast, very

INTERNATIONAL DEBUT:
VS. SCOTLAND 1986

CAPS:
20

POSITION:
BLIND-SIDE FLANKER

powerful, dynamic player – which is exacly what is

required nowadays. He also had great ball handling skills.

Jon was never a headline winner but more often than not he was his team's saviour. He was one of the supreme athletes but has simply been very, very unlucky with injuries. He was always very strong mentally, however. He was one of the most consistent players I have come across. He had a valiant 'never say die' attitude to the game, and I have always admired him for his staying power.

In Jon Hall, I have a player who performed at the very highest level of international rugby, despite injury, for more than 10 years. You have to admire someone who put in as much effort and energy and attitude as he did year after year.

Jon Hall continued a remarkable family tradition when he burst into Bath's all-conquering team in the early 1980s. His father Harry and his grandfather Harry Vowles had both played with distinction for the West Country club. They would have been proud of the latest offspring – because Hall developed into a towering back row forward, a player who combined indomitable courage and sure handling ability with a razor-sharp rugby brain.

Speak to any of his colleagues at Bath who played alongside him throughout the glory years and they will say, to a man, that the player with the baby face was the most vital component of their multi-talented team. That cherubic countenance masked a mental and physical toughness. At 6ft 3in and 16½ stone, he was a giant who could play Number Eight or blind side flanker with equal aplomb. He had few equals when it came to the ability to read a game — and to lead a team.

England's selectors saw his potential when they called him up to face Scotland at Murrayfield in 1984 when he was just 21 years old. Even in defeat,

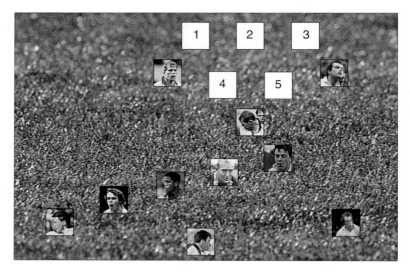

his performance showed a maturity which belied his years. He looked destined to hold his place for the next decade.

Sadly, injuries blighted his career, especially at the very top level. He played only 20 times for England before he was finally forced to quit the international stage in 1990-91 after suffering a knee cartilage injury during the Five Nations Championship training in Lanzarote. He had, typically, already displayed enormous courage to force his way into the side which thumped Argentina 51-0 earlier that season. But he was just not fit enough to survive the rigours of a Championship.

That wasn't the end of his club career, however. He captained Bath to more league championship and cup final triumphs before he finally called it a day. And his club thought so highly of him that he was made team manager when Jack Rowell left them to take over as England supremo.

Even amid the hurly-burly of a game lurching towards professionalism, Hall still retains a warm sense of humour. And he's not afraid to laugh at himself. When asked his most embarrassing moment, he recalled an England Under-23 trial in which he played on a pitch at Bisham Abbey which also had soccer markings: 'I ran to the try-line and triumphantly touched down. Then I discovered I was five metres short!'

PAUL ACKFORD

I realise my side is blessed with some fine talent. But in Paul Ackford, I believe I have my secret weapon! I have opted to play Paul as middle jumper, wearing the Number Five shirt – and I'm sure (or at least I hope) that Martin Bayfield will understand!

Ackford is a tactician: a thinker as well as a player. He is very athletic and a good handler, always looking supremely confident and comfortable with the ball in his hand.

Although he came late to international rugby, he made a great impression on me – and everyone else. He was the middle jumper for the Harlequins when he came back, for almost a one-off game, in 1992 and he was brilliant. He proved himself a very intelligent player, a great lineout forward.

When considering my selection, I always had in mind which players could perform the kind of rugby that is need-

INTERNATIONAL DEBUT:
VS. AUSTRALIA **1988**

CAPS:
22

POSITION:
LOCK

ed today. I am confident that Ackford could perform as middle jumper today just as well as he used to do for the Harlequins.

He would give a depth of experience to the side and would offer a lot of thought in the build-up to game – and even more to the game itself.

The story of how Paul Ackford took a decade to become an overnight success has been told frequently as he enjoyed an Indian summer in his career.

He played for England B in 1979, but it was only in 1988 that he won his first cap, when the knowledge that he had not done himself justice stirred him mightily. In Australia with the 1989 Lions, Ackford was still in his first international season, yet he was a key figure.

As a police inspector, he had a natural air of authority about him. Being 6ft 8in tall reinforced it. During the tour and in his subsequent England games, he was THE productive source of possession at the front of the line-out. And at the kick-off and drop-out he was regarded by the Aussies as one of the hardest, harshest Lions ever.

Paul carried on this late and spectacular progress in the famous 1989-90 season, when he was 32 years of age. Memorably, he brought off an astonishing tackle on Philippe Sella, the French centre, when he appeared near the wing during the British Isles match against France in Paris, an event widely replayed on television.

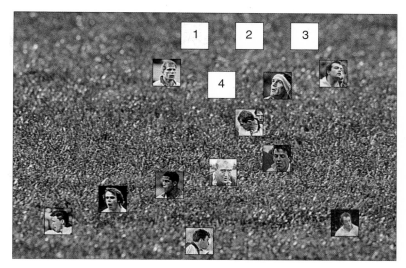

He was at the heart of England's Grand Slam years, unerring at the front of the line-out and a massive force in the loose in tandem with his partner, PC Wade Dooley – the Blackpool Tower. His form during that period makes him a natural for selection in any World XV, let alone a Will Carling one.

Paul John Ackford, born in Hannover, Germany, in 1958, made Harlequins his club. Ironically, he now makes more money than he ever did as rugby correspondent of *The Sunday Telegraph* and is a regular TV pundit at the Five Nations and at the last World Cup.

He is also remembered for being on the receiving end of a mighty right hook from Argentine prop forward Federico Mendez. It was at Twickenham in 1990 when the young Argie, barely 17, went into the history books as the youngest player ever to be sent off in rugby union. He had boxing promoters beating a path to his door after delivering a punch the like of which London hadn't seen since Our 'Enery put Cassius Clay onto the canvas in the 1960's.

Argentina were on their way to a 51-0 hammering, when England's wily prop of the day, Jeff Probyn, appeared to stamp on Mendez's head. 'He was so wound up I knew it would take little to push him over the top,' Probyn recalls. 'We were in the last quarter of the game when we wheeled a scrum and they collapsed. We drove on and I stepped on him as we did so. He swung a fist at me and then tried to grab my testicles. I trod on the side of his head. Mendez curled his fist and lashed out at the first person he saw, which was Paul Ackford. As Ackers had his back to the boy, he was the only person in the ground who didn't see the punch coming and it landed on the side of his jaw, putting him out cold. Exit Mendez and Ackford.'

Mendez was banned from the game for four weeks. But at the after-match banquet, Ackford's wife took pity on Mendez, who was so ashamed that he sat alone. She gathered England autographs and handed them to the youngster. A year later, Inspector Ackford met Mendez again and presented the trainee lawyer with one of his helmets.

'He is a very nice man and I treasure the helmet,' says Mendez. 'I keep it in a special place at home. I have had no more trouble in the game since that day. Now I am the captain of my club and I do not punch people any more. Ackford is one of the greatest players I have ever met, and I do not want to be remembered as the man who knocked him out. I felt very bad about it.'

MARTIN JOHNSON

At Number Four, I have made what many rugby watchers will consider to be a surprise selection. I was spoiled for choice for my front jumper, as names like Maurice Colclough must always be in the frame. Instead, I have chosen Martin Johnson.

Martin is actually a very good athlete and very committed. It has been said (but not by me) that he is an over-committed player, in the way he can give a penalty away. But I think he's excellent in the lineout. He is a supreme athlete and makes some big tackles – getting hold of the ball and taking it forward.

He is a great tactical thinker and seems to turn up suddenly in the right place on the field to make the perfect tackle. The game is more and more about broken field situations and players who can 'read' that sort of game – and Martin can.

INTERNATIONAL DEBUT:
VS. FRANCE 1993

CAPS:
19

POSITION:
LOCK

He is a dynamic player who does a lot of good work all over the pitch. Modern rugby – and the way it is evolving – needs players like Martin Johnson.

Johan Le Roux's rasping right hook left more than a lasting impression on Martin Johnson… it left him looking for the first flight home to England. It was the moment the Leicester lock realised that you need eyes in the back and sides of your head to succeed in international rugby.

Johnson's pride was hurt more than his body as he lay there on the Transvaal pitch in 1994, half unconscious and wishing he'd taken a leaf out of his predecessor's book. PC Wade Dooley was the master at dodging flying fists — as fellow policeman Paul Ackford found out to his dismay against Argentina at Twickenham. But Martin Johnson obviously had not learnt the lesson of being a high-profile, highly dangerous opponent. Perhaps he should have listened to the cries of 'Watch out' from parts of the stadium as the game descended into violence.

Having been helped off on that unfortunate day in South Africa, Johnson knew his tour was over. He admits: 'I couldn't remember what happened or who did it. And I certainly didn't see the punch coming. Otherwise I would have got

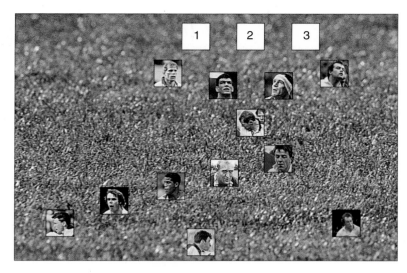

out the way.

Loss of memory is one of the symptoms that convinced the medical team that I was concussed. I had had about a year at the top, being in the England team and with a couple of Tests with the Lions. Then the bubble suddenly burst.'

Johnson, however, picked himself up, dusted himself down and – niggling injuries aside – continued to prove himself as England's prized front-line jumper. He had huge and daunting footsteps to follow in. But his partnership with Martin Bayfield is still blossoming into one of the best in the world, continuing England's proud conveyer belt of lock pairings. Bill Beaumont and Maurice Colclough, and Wade Dooley and Paul Ackford,

will vouch for that.

Johnson grabbed his chance of international glory when Dooley had to withdraw through injury on the eve of the clash with France in 1993. In that incredible year, Martin helped Leicester win the Pilkington Cup and took injured Dooley's Lions spot.

During the last two years, Johnson has grown in stature and maturity on the field. The 1995 World Cup semi-final with New Zealand was one of his worst performances in an England shirt. But, then again, which of Will Carling's men could hold their heads up high after that Kiwi drubbing?

Johnson will, no doubt, bounce back with a vengeance. He's still only 25 and time is on his side.

JASON LEONARD

My Number Three is Jason Leonard. He's a player who was capped in his early twenties but who continues to go from strength to strength. Jason is still learning and the efforts of players like him often go unnoticed. But I've put him in

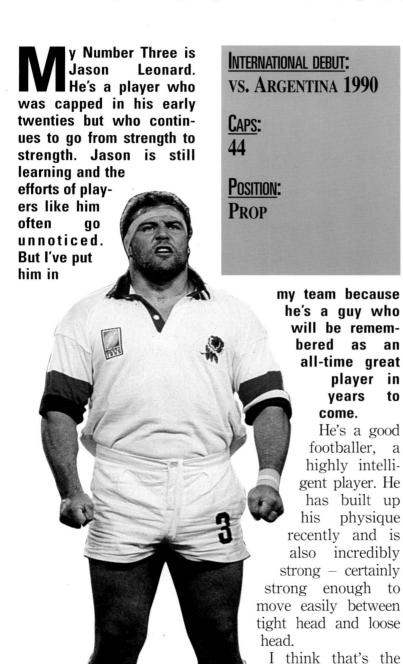

INTERNATIONAL DEBUT:
VS. ARGENTINA 1990

CAPS:
44

POSITION:
PROP

my team because he's a guy who will be remembered as an all-time great player in years to come.

He's a good footballer, a highly intelligent player. He has built up his physique recently and is also incredibly strong – certainly strong enough to move easily between tight head and loose head.

I think that's the way with top men.

They are actually so good, so strong, that you can play them either way. Although the forwards will be going berserk that I've said that!

Jason keeps telling me how good he is in the scrummage and I wouldn't dare disagree with him! But for me, it's his handling that shines out every time he plays. He's a great ball handler, great out on the pitch. And he's very good in the lineout.

The future of English rugby is bright as long as talent such as Jason's, is continually discovered.

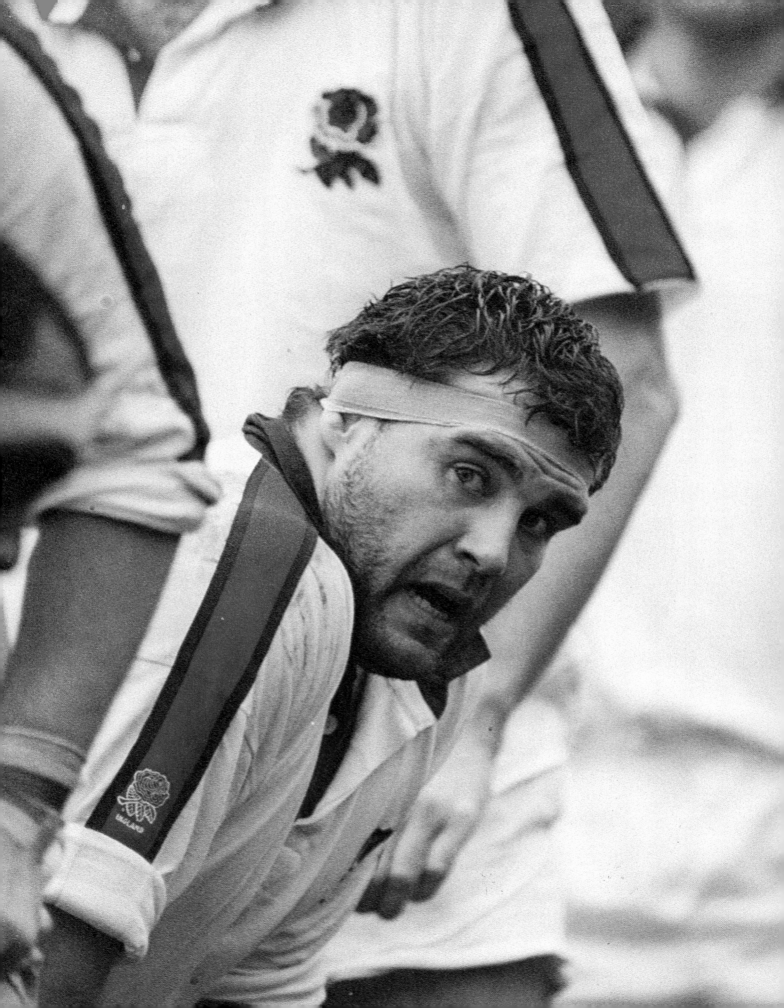

To his friends, Jason Leonard is known as 'Mr Quiet' or 'Mr Reliable' – the unsung hero of English rugby's recent glory years. To his enemies, he's simply 'Mr Muscles' – the strong-armed, no-nonsense prop who is as hard as nails and just as painful if you happen to get on the wrong end.

Essex man 'Jase' is also a record breaker who knows he's lucky to be alive. Three and a half years ago, the Harlequins ace had his career almost halted in mid-flow when he broke a bone in his neck during a game. It was the sudden clicking sound and tingling feeling down his spine which told Leonard that something serious had happened. He certainly feared the worst on that day back in 1992 when his future was left dangling by a thread. Surgeons had to drill through the windpipe and used a piece of bone from his thigh to repair the damage to the ruptured disc in his neck.

Fortunately, the fears for his future were quickly defused but he still suffered the kind of injury that could have broken the heart and spirit of most rugby mortals. Had he listened to medical experts then, he would

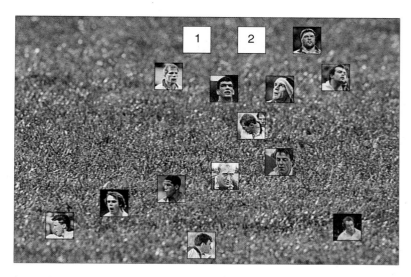

have hung up his boots. But Leonard, one of the real hard men of the game, who puts the fear of God in his rivals with his silent, menacing character, defied the doctors and has gone on to achieve true greatness.

He admits: 'When I was 21, I got my first cap and everyone was saying, "You'll have a good ten years or so with England and break all sorts of records." But then I hurt my neck and I realised that you can't take anything for granted. That could easily have finished me.'

The rewards for his rugby bravery beyond the cause of duty have been to play in three England Grand Slam winning sides, a World Cup Final and a Pilkington Cup Final for Harlequins. Jason, a sales

manager, also got on the British Lions tour to New Zealand a year after the neck injury.

And running out to face the auld enemy in that 1994 Grand Slam encounter at Twickenham, Leonard wrote his own personal place in the rugby union history books by becoming England's most capped prop. It was his 38th appearance in the white shirt.

Who knows how many more caps and honours he will win with both England and the British Lions. At 27, he still has many more years at the top ahead of him. He will still be in the running when the next World Cup comes around in 1999.

PETER WHEELER

The hooker in my Dream Team will be Peter Wheeler. I feel that anyone who wants to play hooker – suspended between two huge guys and at the mercy of everyone else – must have

INTERNATIONAL DEBUT:
VS. FRANCE 1975

CAPS:
41

POSITION:
HOOKER

something seriously wrong with them up top! But I have to say that, in every sense, Peter was all there.

I used to study his play and came to realise just how committed he was. Peter was a crucial character in the 1980 Grand Slam team. He was respected by his colleagues and by the opposition. His peers recognised him as a great technical player, as a hooker and for his throwing in. And we all know how crucial that is.

You can sense the players whom people respect, and he was certainly one of them. He was also a great motivator – and he would display the same virtue in my Dream Team – geeing up the lads and ensuring that morale never drops.

Above all, I chose him because he has to be one of the most committed players rugby has ever seen. Peter, you have to be in this side!

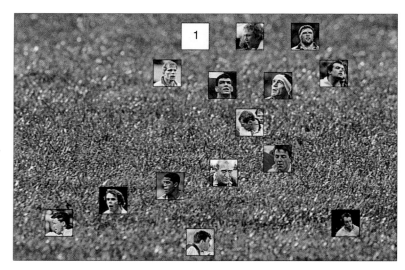

As well as proving himself one of the outstanding hookers in the world in his era, Peter Wheeler was also one of the greatest captains of all time. He led Leicester through nearly a decade of sensational success. But he had to wait eight years to get the chance to captain England. He made his debut in 1975 but it was not until 1983, when he was 35 years old, that the selectors finally entrusted him with the leadership.

Wheeler's response was dramatic. He immediately led England to a stunning victory over New Zealand – their first against the fabled All Blacks at Twickenham for 47 years.

Wheeler, a dynamic and natural leader, was worshipped by those who played under him. But he was often an outspoken critic of the way the game was organised in England in his playing years. And the chaps at the RFU may just have been a trifle reluctant to hand the skipper's mantle to a man who might have caused them the odd problem off the field.

Peter did play under a couple of great leaders in his early days with England, however. Roger Uttley was the captain when he came

into the side, and he was succeeded by the immortal Bill Beaumont. But when Beaumont departed, Steve Smith and John Scott were both given the job before Wheeler's belated call. Had he been handed the role a year or two earlier, he would surely have gone on to win the highest honour of all — captaincy of the British Lions team in New Zealand.

The Lions selectors have always opted for an internationally-proven leader. So they plumped instead for Ireland's Ciaran Fitzgerald. That meant, with Fitzgerald also a hooker, that Wheeler couldn't even fight for a place in the Test team. But he did play in seven Tests for the Lions, all told, to add to his total of 41 England caps. Wheeler had to see off the great Welshman, Bobby

Windsor, to win his first Lions call, in New Zealand in 1977. That was when he really announced his presence on the world stage.

Wheeler remains deeply involved in rugby, as president of Leicester and chairman of the First Division clubs. That makes him a leading figure in the switch towards professionalism. It also means that the man once considered too much of a rebel for Twickenham's liking is now telling THEM what to do! And that will amuse him greatly.

FRAN COTTON

When it comes to scrummaging, I'm a totally ignorant and a willing bystander! So when it came to placing a name by the side of the Number One position, I opted for experience, size – and the great Fran Cotton.

I never saw Fran play live or played against him (thank goodness!) but I well remember watching him in action on television. His determination and tackling were renowned. He was always very alert and aware of everything that was going on around him. He was then able to judge

INTERNATIONAL DEBUT:
VS. SCOTLAND 1971

CAPS:
30

POSITION:
PROP

how and when to lend his support where it mattered most.

He was picked for all the Lions Tours and

you cannot buy experience like that. He was a huge man and an awesome player.

Every team needs a Fran Cotton and the flair players in my side will be relieved that I have chosen him as my prop.

Fran Cotton was born to be a star... of rugby league! He came rampaging into this world at Wigan in 1948. His father David was already a well-known rugby league player with Warrington. But Fran had to switch to union when he won a place at Newton le Willows Grammar School.

Fran began to reach national prominence when he was a star with Loughborough College. And he pulled an England jersey over that famous lantern jaw for the first time against Scotland at Twickenham in 1971. It wasn't a memorable debut. The Scots triumphed at HQ for the first time since World War 2.

Cotton had to wait two years for his next chance. By then he had matured into his full 6ft 2in, 17-stone frame. He kept his place throughout the Five Nations campaign and then starred in their historic victory over New Zealand at Auckland later in the same year.

England's fortunes were very mixed in those days, with startling glories contrasting with dismal performances against opposition that should have been beaten. But Cotton was a model of strength and consistency amid the general medi-

ocrity. It earned him seven British Lions Test caps against New Zealand and South Africa alongside the 30 times he played for his country, right up to 1981.

Cotton's old league background helped to make him far more than just a powerhouse in the scrum. He loved to run with the ball, and when he broke into full awesome flight it took a brave man to halt him.

Sadly, his career was hampered by injuries. Both knees were damaged by the wear and tear of scrummaging; he suffered constant Achilles tendon problems; he even dislocated a shoulder. And his Lions tour to South Africa in 1980 was curtailed when he discovered he had heart trouble.

A few months before that stunning blow, Fran had achieved his major ambition: helping England to a notable Grand Slam, under the captaincy of his close pal Bill Beaumont. Even the heart fear did not prevent Cotton from forcing his way back into England's team next season. But a leg injury kept him off the field during the game with Wales in Cardiff. That was to be his international farewell.

Perhaps the most glowing tribute he ever earned came from his England and Lions colleague Peter Wheeler when the heart ailment was first diagnosed. Dr Christian Barnard, the eminent heart surgeon, jokingly offered Cotton a new heart. 'You could search every country in the world and you still wouldn't find a heart big enough to replace Fran's,' said Wheeler.

65

WILL CARLING'S DREAM TEAM

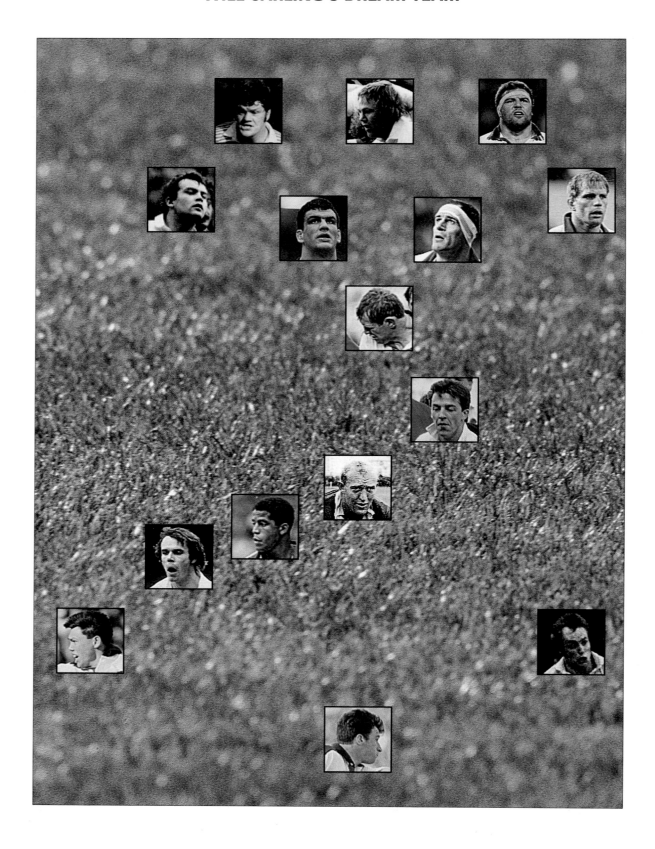

CONCLUSION

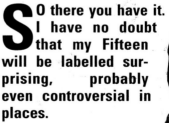

SO there you have it. I have no doubt that my Fifteen will be labelled surprising, probably even controversial in places.

But this is a super team that would certainly scare rigid almost any International side in living memory.

My tactics would be to ensure that the scrummaging and lineouts were perfect and to see that the ball was in the hand as much as humanly possible.

My backs have great pace — and how any side could think of defending against 'Dai' Duckham, Underwood and Catt I have no idea!

With the services of Melville, we will be able to get the ball away very quickly from set pieces.

But above all, I see my team as a very good broken-field side, and that is where its real strength lies.

Selecting my all-time England team has been very difficult. I will have upset some present-day colleagues and perhaps overlooked one or two players from the distant past.

However, it has been great fun. As I look down my team list, I can visualise them out there as a unit.

So that is Will Carling's Dream Team ... a force to be reckoned with!

With disarming candour, Clive Woodward provides us with the photograph (right) and the following description of what he describes as 'the worst moment in my entire rugby career'.

The picture was taken during a Wales versus England match on 17 January 1981 when, according to a contemporary report, 'the Welsh back row conspired to lure Woodward off-side at a scrummage in injury time and Fenwick landed the penalty goal'. Wales thereby won by 21 to 19.

Clive Woodward writes: 'If I ever need cheering up, I still look at this photograph - with the caption "Things Can Only Get Better!"

'England had not beaten Wales in Cardiff for 18 years, since 1963.

'In injury time, England were winning 19-18 when inexplicably I was lured off-side to hand Wales the match with a penalty from 20 metres in front of the posts.

'This was quite simply the worst moment in my rugby career.

'The photograph was taken the very instant that the referee blew his whistle penalising me.

'To all my team mates on that day, my sincere apologies!

"I would like to express my gratitude to Will for the compliment which he has paid me. Like Will Carling, I had the pleasure of leading England to success in the Home Unions Championship and I have great admiration for the achievements of the England team in recent years under his captaincy.'

Sharp is most often reminded of his try against Scotland in 1963, which won the match for England. But he says: 'My greatest match for England was against Ireland the year before, when we won by 16 points to nil. I scored 10 points, including a try under the posts in the closing minutes - to make it a day to remember'.

Richard Sharp

PAUL ACKFORD'S REACTION

"Will Carling is at it again - controversial, indiscreet, provocative. Only this time it is all good clean fun. The Dream Team he has chosen is interesting because it reveals a great deal about Carling's rugby philosophy: the qualities he most admires in others and the state of the game today. I offer you (from my *Daily Telegraph* column) a few personal observations."

MIKE CATT: He has marked time recently and his selection illustrates why this is the weakest position in English rugby history.

DAVID DUCKHAM: Carling describes him as 'very graceful for a big man', good news for Ian Hunter who is the closest thing size-wise at the moment. Tony Underwood should get stuck into his pizza!

JEREMY GUSCOTT: Carling must be thinking of Guscott's exploits five or six years ago, but the choice smashes the theory that the two men do not get on.

CLIVE WOODWARD: How Carling describes him is just about the epitaph he would choose for himself when he steps down.

RORY UNDERWOOD: He may put the fear of God into the opposition, as Carling says, but also, on one or two occasions, he puts the fear of God into his own team.

RICHARD SHARP: How sad Carling has to retreat to the 1960s to find his playmaker; how sad that Sharp's philosophy ('a man whose first instinct was to run') makes Sharp's philosophy almost untenable.

NIGEL MELVILLE: Remember the days when brain beat brawn, skill overcame strength? The most famous player in world rugby today is Jonah Lomu. Enough said.

DEAN RICHARDS: Even though Richards' limitations are increasingly exposed, Carling still wants him. There is obviously more to the man than a rolling maul.

PETER WINTERBOTTOM: Carling says he 'couldn't conceive of fielding a team without him'. Me neither. The best forward of his generation. Possibly ever.

JON HALL: Carling is no mug. With Hall completing a formidable back row, there would be no need for any of the backs to get their hands dirty.

PAUL ACKFORD: Now you know why I'm plugging this!

MARTIN JOHNSON: Of whom Carling says 'supreme athlete - very dynamic'.

JASON LEONARD: Whose 'handling shines out': Both strong, silent types. No good on chat shows, but very articulate at the bottom of a ruck.

PETER WHEELER: Strange that Carling should select Wheeler ahead of Brian Moore, who also has a reputation in both areas he describes ('a great motivator and one of the most committed players rugby has ever seen'). Maybe Moore has said something recently.

FRAN COTTON: One of the few forwards of the 1970s who would be at home in the 1990s. Owner of the most famous chin in rugby.

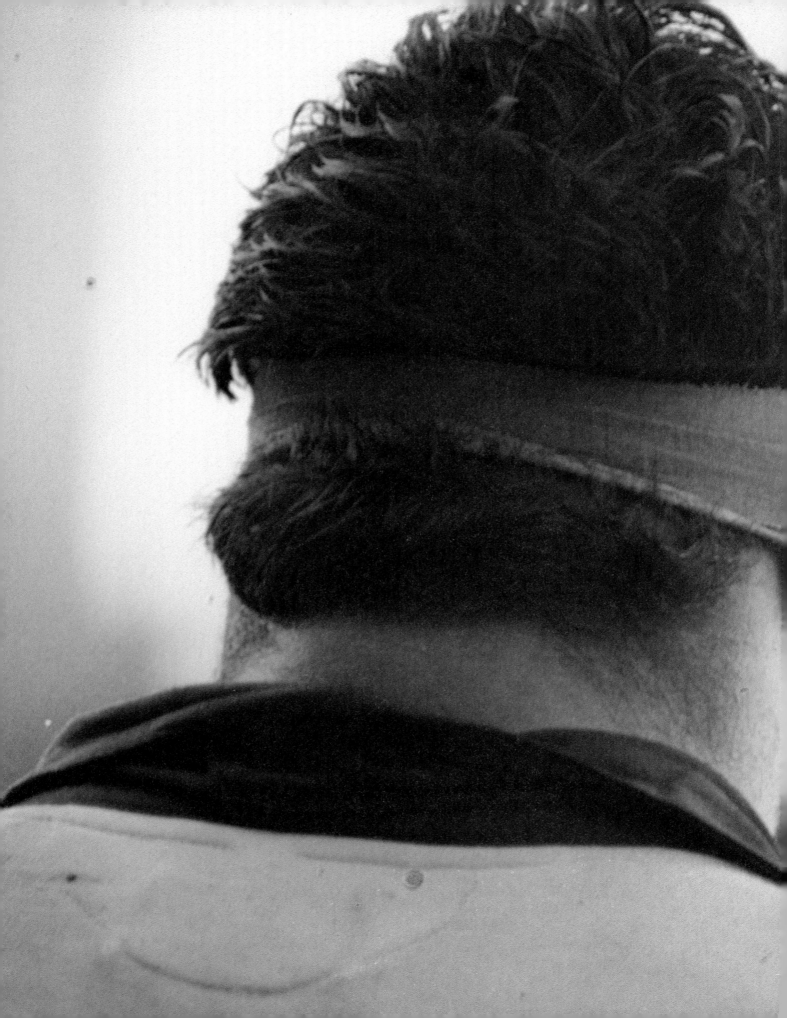

index